ONE SIMPLE STEP

EMOTIONAL HEALING THE EASY WAY

BETH KEARNEY

BALBOA.PRESS

A DIVISION OF HAY HOUSE

Balboa Press books may be ordered through booksellers or by contacting:

Balboa Press
A Division of Hay House
1663 Liberty Drive
Bloomington, IN 47403
www.balboapress.co.uk
UK TFN: 0800 0148647 (Toll Free inside the UK)
UK Local: (02) 0369 56325 (+44 20 3695 6325 from outside the UK)

Print information available on the last page.

ISBN: 978-1-9822-8908-9 (sc)
ISBN: 978-1-9822-8907-2 (hc)
ISBN: 978-1-9822-8906-5 (e)

Library of Congress Control Number: 2024919057

Balboa Press rev. date: 12/13/2024

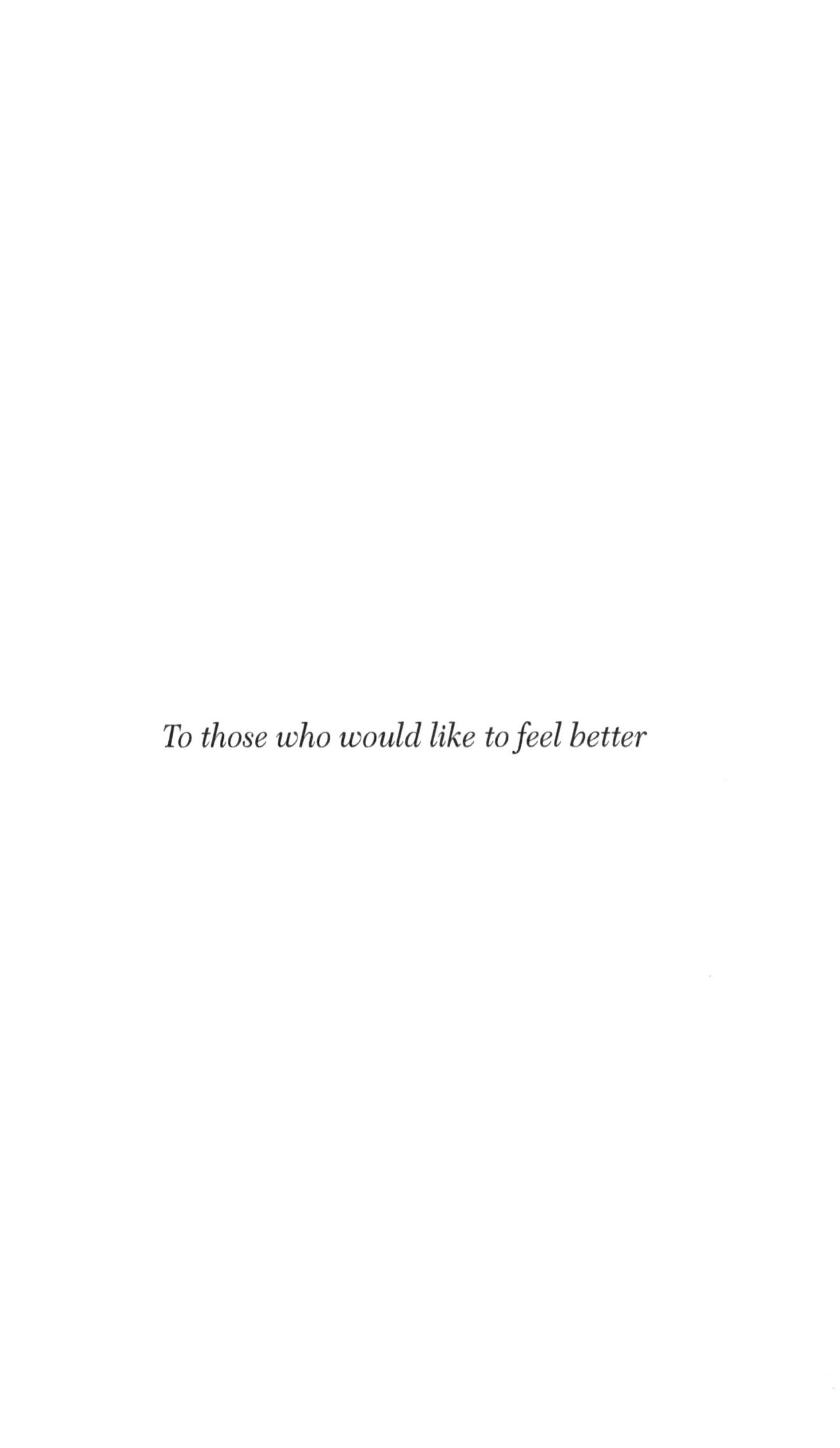

To those who would like to feel better

Attune yourself to the wisdom of your emotions.

Reduce anxiety, stress, worries, unhelpful
thoughts and unhelpful beliefs.

Increase ease, clarity, well-being, inner
peace, energy and motivation.

Gain happiness and a healthy and robust degree
of self-esteem, self-worth and self-value.

Gain clarity on what is right and what is wrong for you.

Feel clear in body and mind.

Live more in the present.

Heal the past.

Forgive.

Your mind becomes calmer, appreciation and gratitude
become effortless and positive thinking happens naturally.

Align with your true self.

Feel empowered, vibrant, happy and glowing.

Put the simple and straightforward into
living with your emotions.

CONTENTS

ACKNOWLEDGEMENTS

With special thanks and appreciation to:

Sue, Joanna, Martin, and some life experiences,
for pointing out the direction.

Amanda for believing in this book and this method.

Leesa and Zoe for the peer supervision.

One Simple Step provides a new psychology on how you can avoid the pitfalls of unhelpful thinking and enable more opportunities for feeling happy.

DISCLAIMER

If you have been living with emotional difficulties and choose to utilise the information within these pages, circumstances in your life may be revealed that are out of harmony with who you truly are. How you respond to those circumstances is your choice and up to your discretion and is not the responsibility of the author.

One Simple Step is a guide on how to understand the guidance of your negative emotions. With this information, you can clear unnecessary emotional suffering from your life if you want to.

If you are the captain of your ship, then negative emotions can be seen as part of your crew. They provide valuable information to assist you in navigating life whilst you, as captain, are the overseer of the bigger picture and remain the decision-maker.

One Simple Step is not intended for those with psychosis or for those experiencing symptoms that would be diagnosed as psychosis. Also, this method is not suitable for those living with PTSD or experiencing ongoing uncontrollable and unwanted thoughts.

PART I
INTRODUCTION

CHAPTER 1
INTRODUCTION

When I branched out on this mission, I believed the path to emotional healing was a process that takes time. I thought I was searching for a system an individual moves through with the expertise of another.

Instead, my search has led me to a few pieces of information on negative emotions.

When we understand our emotions from this simple framework, the old paradigm of how to work with emotional issues is turned on its head and we are no longer broken or need fixing.

If I had known this mission of mine was going to take me down a rabbit hole of unhappiness for years though, I would not have pursued it. However, it was early on in this journey that I learnt the glorious benefits of this simple one-step method. And how easy, efficient and effective the emotional healing that is gained, when we use this framework to understand what the body is communicating through the channel we call emotions.

It turns out the best foundation to greater happiness and aligning with who you truly are is an understanding of negative emotions. So, here it is. I have kept *One Simple Step* as concise as possible to deliver my message and all you need to know to set yourself free from emotional issues.

The terms *emotional issues* and *unnecessary emotional suffering* are used interchangeably throughout *One Simple Step*.

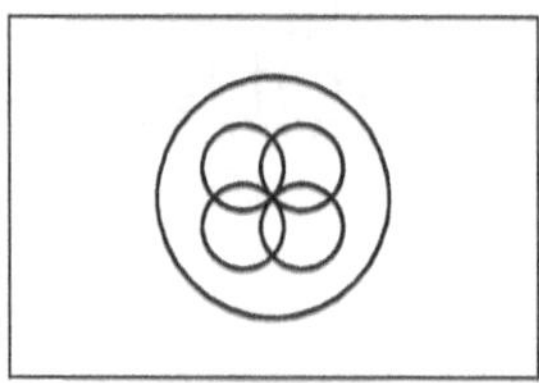

The concepts within these pages are different from how we have traditionally understood emotions and how to heal them.

Traditionally negative emotions have been seen as problems needing to be fixed. We analyse our stories, make conscious efforts to be positive, retrain our thought processes and reframe our mindset. We search for the cause of problems, look for uncomfortable emotions and memories, invite others to do the same and then misinterpret the discomfort which arises from this. Past experiences are worked through and released again and again as we delve ever deeper into traumas and the pain they cause. This can take months, years, or even decades to do. Yet the desired healing is never complete: old wounds are reopened and judging from the pandemics of anxiety and depression we see today, the emotional discomfort continues to shout and shouts ever louder.

From my early teens and up until I began using this method, I lived with anxiety, low self-esteem, unhelpful self-beliefs and self-defeating habitual thought patterns. For years before I embarked on this therapeutic journey and whilst I was on it, my natural default place to reside, the feeling state I always sprang back to, was anxiety and a feeling of disempowerment.

Now that I have discovered the information I present to you in *One Simple Step*, my natural place to reside is clarity and happiness. I now understand the language of my feelings and the storm has made way for a new calm and greater simplicity.

I spent years searching for a way to heal my emotional wounds. Understanding my negative emotions from this framework, which leads to the practice of this one-step method, works wonders for me. It is the easiest, quickest and most efficient, effective, enjoyable, thorough, complete and beneficial path to emotional healing that I have used.

So it is with a heartfelt desire that I present to you my theory and the culmination of my research.

Because we learn best through experience, I invite you to hold this information up against your own emotions. Trial it and see if it holds true for you. If it does, then you have all the information you need to make many and varied improvements to your emotional well-being and you can do this with one simple, quick and easy step that is also in harmony with the wisdom of your body.

One Simple Step is a guide on how to understand the guidance of negative emotions.

However, you are the captain of your ship, so negative emotions are to be seen as part of your crew. They provide valuable information to assist you in navigating life whilst you, as captain, are the overseer of the bigger picture and remain the decision-maker.

CHAPTER 2
SOME OF THE BENEFITS

With this model, there is no need to develop greater awareness of your thoughts or your emotions. There is no need to try to describe and translate them into words, or analyse them, or work out where patterns and beliefs originated. There is no need to dig deep and search for hidden and underlying issues. There is no working through of emotional difficulties and no need to be a detective in any way regarding your psyche.

There is no need to override your thoughts and emotions so that they fit with what another thinks they should be.

There are no hidden or unresolved traumas to identify and there is no need to avoid, suppress, or change negative emotions. Instead, these emotions disappear and evaporate with ease, revealing greater clarity of your true self and direction.

Reconciliation is made with the past, without the need to revisit or release old problems. Forgiveness occurs, as does healing of the inner child, without the need to consciously engage with the process. Mistakes and hurt are no longer dragged from the past into the present; flaws recede and the beauty surfaces; and each individual is empowered to know what is right and what is wrong for him or her, as no other person has this degree of insight into another's emotions.

We are able to banish catastrophic thinking, negative

self-talk and limiting self-beliefs, which then reveals what is out of harmony with our true selves and deserving of our attention.

When we align with the wisdom of our emotions and our own source of truth, issues with low self-esteem, low self-worth, poor body image, jealousy, self-doubt, self-sabotage, unhelpful and unwanted thought patterns, self-defeating beliefs, self-criticism, comparing oneself unfavourably to others and unnecessary fears, unhappiness, worries, anxieties, confusion, stress and doubts all become part of an old world and an old way of being.

Positive thinking, appreciation, the creation and strengthening of healthy self-beliefs, self-trust, inner strength and resilience, greater understanding of who you truly are and happiness are all effortless side effects of this practice.

With the practice of this method, self-growth is an easy, pleasant, positive and often joyful experience and the reality we are creating is better for us and for those we share our lives with. We have greater clarity in mind and body; understanding emotions becomes easy; and tuning into the wisdom from within is simply when we notice we feel either good or bad emotionally.

CHAPTER 3
HOW THIS METHOD WAS DEVELOPED

Since childhood, I have been trying to fathom it out, observing others and myself and trying to figure out why that person behaved like that and why I behaved like this.

When I was 22, I came across books on self-healing, which I was immediately drawn to. Eleven years later (2004), I started my training in hypnotherapy and knew I had found my niche. I devoured my training books and so many more, paid full attention to the course, practised the techniques and continued to learn beyond my initial training. I set up my hypnotherapy practice in 2009. The financial reward this work gave me, though, was telling me to change direction. Yet I felt compelled to continue.

I have been driven forward by my beliefs that self-healing is possible and that there must surely be an easy way to tap into the health, well-being and happiness of who we truly are. I feel this to be true at my core, even though the world around me is telling me a different story.

I learnt how to meditate and clear my mind of thoughts. A journey of learning and of practising many different healing and therapeutic approaches, together with years of quietening my mind, pointed me in the direction of finding my answer. I continued searching the various therapies out there for that easier solution I knew I needed to find. Like stepping stones, those therapies led me in the direction I needed to go and opened my mind to possibilities.

In summer 2016, I started to get inspired ideas of ways I could bring the beliefs I held into a better feeling place. A light beamed from within me when those ideas started flowing into my mind and I knew I had the beginnings of a healing system. I practised the method I was developing and used myself as a trial case. Several months later, a friend, Amanda and I decided to have a go and see if this method could assist her too. I knew how much it was helping me; I believed in it; and Amanda believed in me.

By summer 2017, I was ready to invite several other friends to hear about this method and they all volunteered to come along for sessions and give the method a go. This venture proved as exciting as I thought it would be, with many sessions confirming my new beliefs created over the previous year that therapeutic change can be pleasant and even joyful.

Sessions were under way and so too was *One Simple Step*.

I was discovering a different way of understanding the psyche, emotions and behaviours from what I had been trained in and what I was discovering was so much more beautiful and succinct.

I gradually suspended what I had learnt about emotional healing from my previous training. Over the course of a couple of years, I then brought my traditional hypnotherapy sessions to an end, closed business on a more spiritual type of hypnotherapy, realised *One Simple Step* was all that was required to practise this method, brought those sessions to a close also, returned to office work and continued with this mission, working on it whenever and as often as I could.

Those around me were actively enjoying life, making progress and achieving. From the outside, I was doing little of this and to some it probably seemed that I was doing little of anything. I minimised external distractions, noise, information and input whenever possible and instead tuned inwards and listened to the inner voice of my feelings.

I continually observed my emotion response to my interactions with others and to my own thoughts and behaviours. I observed. I posed questions. Answers sometimes came into my thoughts, often when I awoke in the morning. Sometimes everyday experiences gave me clues, sometimes even my dreams at night — and *One Simple Step* steadily evolved alongside my understanding of the psyche and healing as I gradually found and put the pieces of this puzzle together.

I held what I was discovering up against my own experiences, and what I observed in others, and found it to be true again and again.

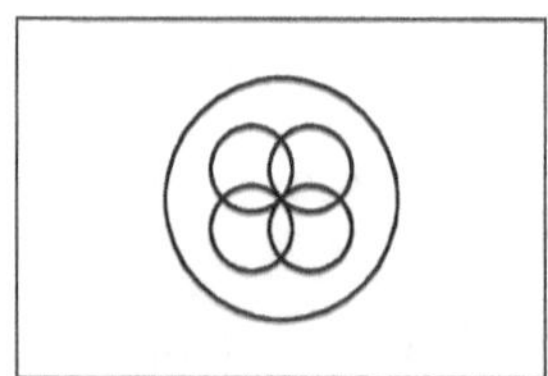

Throughout the following section, I discuss the four units of the psyche as presented within this model, which are (1) emotions, (2) the conscious and subconscious, (3) beliefs and (4) thoughts.

There are several threads of discussion in Part II. However, there is no need for you to struggle to hold onto them. Instead, they are summarised in bold through the chapters of Part II and then the main eight threads are brought together in the chapter titled 'Framework for Understanding Emotions'.

Part II provides the information for understanding the psyche and emotions. In Part III, I condense this into three concise points and take a look at what happens, which is the simple one-step method, when we understand our emotions in this way.

Eight concise points, condensed into three, leads to one simple step and emotional healing the easy way.

All other sections of *One Simple Step* support Part III and explain how this method works, how it was developed, some of the benefits of this method, why the benefits are effortless side effects of the method, how we got ourselves into such a pickle in the first place and when and why the practice of this method becomes ineffective.

I shall start our tour of the psyche then with emotions and, in the next chapter, look at the relationship between emotions and the true self.

PART II
A NEW UNDERSTANDING

CHAPTER 4

EMOTIONS AND THE TRUE SELF

Our emotions and our true self are inextricably linked.

Emotions tell us if whatever and whomever we are interacting with — from the outside world and also our own internal world of thoughts — is in harmony with who we truly are or not.

Just as our senses and nervous system continually give us feedback on the safety of our physical self, our **emotions** continually give us feedback on the safety of our **true self.** This feedback is in relation to what is happening in the present moment.

Positive emotions are effectively our true selves holding up a card which says:

'Yes, please, more of this.'

Negative emotions are effectively our true selves holding up a card which says:

'No, thanks, that is not for me.'

Positive emotions indicate what is right for us, whereas

negative emotions indicate what is not. We all already generally understand emotions in this way.

If living with our emotions is this simple and straightforward though, then where have we been going wrong?

It is in the chapters titled 'Value of Misalignment', 'Threats to the True Self' and 'Magnetic Force and Illusion of Emotions' that I untangle the knot and provide those few pieces of the puzzle.

CHAPTER 5
INTRODUCING ALIGNMENT AND MISALIGNMENT

The line diagram which follows shows some of the emotions we may feel, from deep grief, despair and depression through to hope, joy and beyond and shows the information from the previous chapter as a diagram. It also introduces the two distinct groups of misalignment and alignment which are used within *One Simple Step* and shows that the feeling of hope is where misalignment shifts into alignment.

Continuum of Emotions

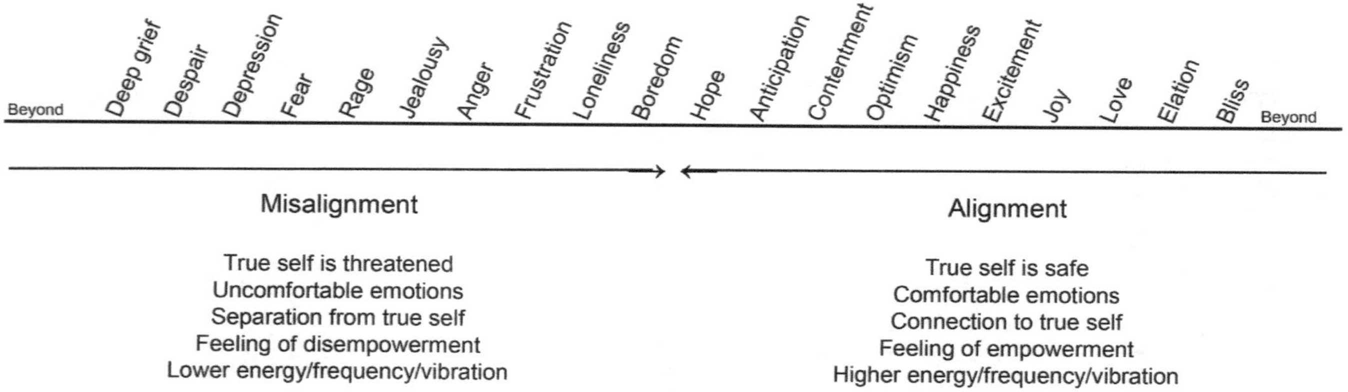

Beyond Deep grief Despair Depression Fear Rage Jealousy Anger Frustration Loneliness Boredom Hope Anticipation Contentment Optimism Happiness Excitement Joy Love Elation Bliss Beyond

Misalignment

True self is threatened
Uncomfortable emotions
Separation from true self
Feeling of disempowerment
Lower energy/frequency/vibration

Alignment

True self is safe
Comfortable emotions
Connection to true self
Feeling of empowerment
Higher energy/frequency/vibration

There are different words for many of the different emotions we may feel. We may also experience feelings and emotions that are difficult to describe in words.

Identifying and describing different emotions is not required for this healing system. Instead, emotions are simply separated into two categories: they feel either comfortable or uncomfortable, they are either aligned or misaligned.

I use the terms *alignment* and *misalignment* throughout *One Simple Step* for purposes of ease, each of these two words referring to a whole host of different feelings.

What is aligned and misaligned for each individual shifts and changes depending upon the shifts and changes of life's circumstances, whilst what is aligned for one person may be misaligned for another.

Life is clear, easy and enjoyable when we feel aligned, whilst it is more complicated, confused and difficult when we feel misaligned. Alignment is energy-giving, whilst misalignment is energy-draining.

CHAPTER 6
ALIGNMENT

Alignment refers to any heart-warming feeling we might describe as positive, good and right.

In addition to good-feeling emotions, alignment brings the clarity, energy and engagement in life which being your true self enables.

Safety of the true self, good feelings and alignment are all one and the same.

When something resonates with us strongly, causing us to light up and making our heart and soul shine, it is because in that moment, the light that we truly are is shining brightly through us and from us.

Our dreams and goals, which fill us with excitement, energy and hope, are dreams and goals that are in alignment. We could have any number of heartfelt dreams across many different areas of interest. In my search for this completed work, I have been following one of mine.

CHAPTER 7
VALUE OF MISALIGNMENT

I shall now look at negative emotions and, by shining a light on what is already commonly understood about them, provide an explanation that reveals their worth.

Misalignment refers to any disheartening feeling we might describe as negative, bad and wrong. In addition to causing bad-feeling emotions, misalignment brings the confusion, lethargy and withdrawal from life which being separated from our true selves causes.

It is uncomfortable, it can be all-encompassing, it can lead to further unhappiness and a downward spiral can ensue. Negative emotions, understandably, have been viewed and treated as the problem because they are uncomfortable to feel.

However, it is not the negative emotion that is the problem, but the cause of the negative emotion.

As already discussed, negative emotions indicate what is not right for us, what is misaligned with our true selves and out of harmony with who we truly are.

Negative emotions can therefore be viewed as a warning signal, an internal alarm, triggered by the wisdom and intelligence of the physiological self when the true self is threatened.

The value of negative emotions is that they are an alarm when there is a threat to the true self.

I use the word *threat* as an umbrella term to describe the many and varied interactions we may have, from minor to extreme and dangerous, that are out of harmony with who we truly are. When I use the word *interaction*, I am referring to anything we interact with, which also includes our own behaviours and our internal world of thoughts.

The true self being threatened, negative emotions and misalignment are all one and the same.

When the alarm of negative emotions is not being triggered, we are in our natural state, which is alignment.

Our natural state is feeling good emotionally. When we feel anything less than hopeful, it is because our physical selves are alerting us to a threat to our true selves.

This chapter provides two points of the framework:

- **Negative emotions are an alarm when the true self is threatened.**

- **When the body is not alerting us to threats, we are in our natural state, which is alignment: the emotions from hope, through to joy and beyond.**

CHAPTER 8
THREATS TO THE TRUE SELF

There are two different types of threat to the true self, which I explain in this chapter, along with providing information on how to distinguish them.

Threats to the true self are either 'false' or 'real'.

False threats exist only when they have our attention. When we turn our attention away from them, they disappear. False threats can include our own thoughts and behaviours.

Real threats in our circumstances exist regardless of where we place our attention and disappear only when they resolve or pass in some way.

False threats exist only when they have our attention.

Real threats exist whether they have our attention or not.

The degree and intensity of negative emotions depends on the cause of the threat and not on whether it is false or real.

False threats can be just as debilitating as real ones and can hold our attention throughout our entire lifetimes, shaping and creating our perceptions, beliefs and reality. When we turn our attention away from a false threat though, the threat no longer exists. The internal alarm is therefore no longer needed and the negative emotions diminish and disappear.

Where there is a real threat, the alarm of negative emotions continues to alert us to it regardless of where we place our attention.

Examples of False Threats and Real Threats

What constitutes a false and a real threat is unique to the individual, his or her story and his or her set of circumstances. The examples provided here are to buttress my explanation and are not intended to override the information any individual is receiving from his or her own emotions.

False Threats
- Self-disapproval and self-deprecation
- A put-down or unhelpful comment from another
- A bad day at work
- An unpleasant atmosphere at home

Real Threats

- Being bullied
- Constant and continuous bad days at work
- Serious financial problems
- Becoming homeless
- Serious health problems of self or a loved one
- An abusive relationship
- Ongoing hard work with little or no time for rest and play

- Self-expression or freedom being stifled or controlled by another
- An ongoing situation where the true self is not recognised or valued

This chapter provides three points of the framework:

- **Threats to the true self are either false or real.**

- **False threats, which can include our own thoughts and behaviours, exist only when they have our attention.**

- **Real threats exist whether they have our attention or not.**

With my explanations of the value of misalignment and how to distinguish false threats from real ones, I have effectively provided the method. However, there is more to understanding the language of emotions before the method can be practised and utilised effectively, which information I provide in the chapter titled 'Magnetic Force and Illusion of Emotions'.

Before moving on to that, I shall look at the conscious, the subconscious, the belief system and thoughts.

The remaining chapters in this section provide the information for understanding how we got ourselves into such a pickle with our emotional health and, by the same token, how the many benefits of practicing this method are natural and effortless side-effects of it.

CHAPTER 9

CONSCIOUS AND SUBCONSCIOUS

Put very simply, the conscious and the subconscious are like a disc.

The outer rim of the disc is the conscious mind, taking in whatever we experience of the world around us through our senses. The vast space within that outer rim is the subconscious, which, like a huge databank, collects and stores this information, keeps it safe and holds it securely along with our automatic responses.

Wherever we are on that outer rim, the wealth of the subconscious is behind us. It holds all the automatic processes of thinking and behaving and of the physical body and it absorbs what we learn.

The conscious and subconscious are one unit working together in unison, each informing and relying upon the other. What we have already learnt informs each moment of each day, whilst each moment of each day also informs our learning. Our learning is the vast wealth of information stored within the subconscious known as the belief system, which I shall look at in greater depth in the following chapter.

The subconscious has traditionally been viewed as an unknown force, submerged like an iceberg, out of sight, yet powerful and influencing us in ways we are unable to control. Viewing the subconscious in this way recognises the vast wealth of information that lies within it and the automatic responses that are driven by it. However, by using the analogy of a disc, we see that the subconscious is no longer lurking out of sight or submerged but is instead right behind the conscious mind.

We absorb the conclusions we form as we face outwards towards the world and experience it.

CHAPTER 10
BELIEF SYSTEM

Beliefs are the attitudes you hold about yourself, others and the world and your place in relation to others and the world. Some of the beliefs we hold are useful and feel good and some are not.

The belief system forms through our experiences, which also includes the beliefs we absorb from those around us and tells us what to expect based on what we and others have already lived. It is the frame of reference we use to make sense of our world and it both mirrors and informs the version of reality we perceive and experience.

The beginnings of the belief system may be likened to the scattering of seeds that grow into a forest. Many different ideas and learnings about many different areas of life set the tone of the belief system that is to grow, just like any seed contains the information for the type of tree that is to grow from it.

With repetition, ideas are gradually absorbed by the subconscious. They take root, form part of the belief system and begin to fuel our thinking patterns. They become part of our perceptions, part of how we see ourselves and our world. With tried-and-tested core beliefs forming, any contradictory idea is more easily rejected.

The reason for this is fundamental to our functioning as living organisms.

What we are learning about ourselves and the world around us needs to be taken on board and accepted as true to assist us in navigating this physical world and remaining physically safe.

Ideas are absorbed within the subconscious regardless of how they feel. It is essential for our survival that we learn what is dangerous as well as what is safe. The way in which our beliefs form helps us navigate this physical life and helps keep us safe and yet, because we absorb ideas regardless of how they feel, our beliefs do not necessarily help keep us emotionally safe. As we experience and learn, we may, without any filters, be absorbing ideas about ourselves which are misaligned and out of harmony with who we truly are.

We experience; we learn; beliefs form through repetition; and we easily reject what does not match those beliefs.

Because of the way we learn and because of this rejecting of what does not match the tried and tested, small seeds of ideas become strong, robust beliefs regardless of whether they are aligned with our true selves or not.

It is our beliefs that fuel our habitual thinking and our habitual thinking in turn, reaffirms and strengthens our beliefs further.

CHAPTER 11
CHATTER OF THE MIND

Unless we are intentionally quietening our minds, we have internal dialogue and a chattering of thoughts meandering and flitting here, there and anywhere.

Thoughts are triggered and fired through our deliberate intention, the triggering of our belief system, memories and imagination. As a backdrop to this, we also form conclusions, whether aligned or misaligned, on whatever we are experiencing, which become additional beliefs.

In the next chapter, I discuss the magnetic force and illusion of emotions and reveal the order that is within this seemingly random and spontaneous chattering of the mind.

The information in the following chapter explains the influence of emotions on our psyche and behaviours, provides the last piece of this puzzle and concludes my explanation of the four units of the psyche.

This chapter, along with the previous two, provides one point of the framework:

-   **Beliefs form through repetition and regardless of how those beliefs feel.**

CHAPTER 12
MAGNETIC FORCE AND ILLUSION OF EMOTIONS

Whatever we are feeling emotionally at any particular time influences the kinds of thoughts we have and also the kinds of thoughts we resonate with and believe.

This magnetic force and illusion causes us to become caught in cycles and loops of thoughts and emotions that are of the same vibration, essence and frequency. This is what I referred to in the previous chapter as the 'order' that is within the seemingly random and spontaneous chatter of the mind.

Add beliefs into the mix and those cycles have even greater power to trap us within them, as illustrated in the following two diagrams:

When we feel aligned

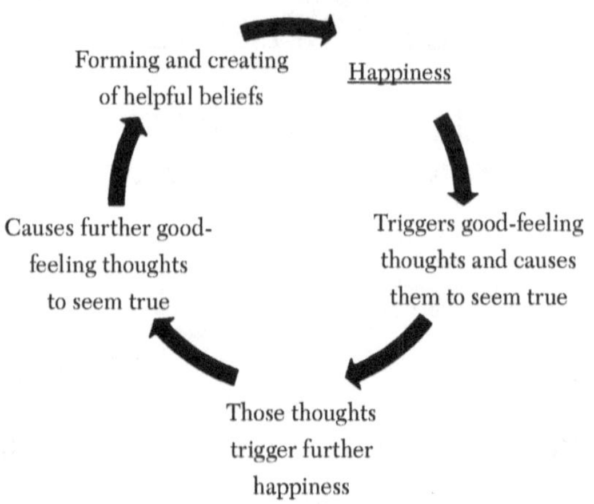

When we feel misaligned

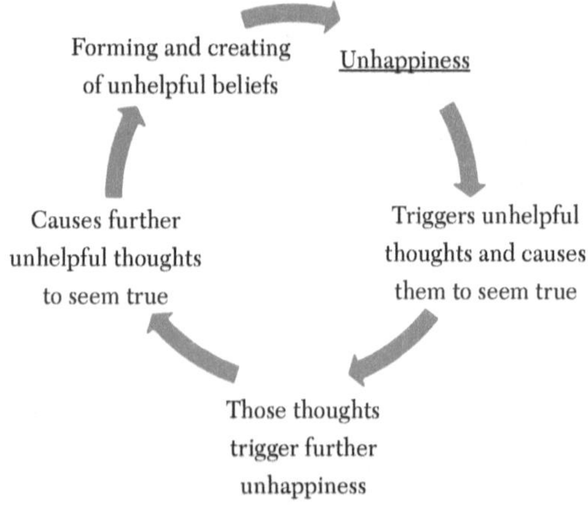

How we feel affects the kinds of thoughts that randomly pop into our minds, the kinds of thoughts and ideas that seem believable, the trains of thought we therefore follow, the beliefs we therefore take on board and all the other experiences of life that ripple out from this.

It is the beliefs we hold, together with the emotion we are feeling, that serve as the lens through which we perceive.

I was trapped by this force and illusion and easily became caught in cycles of faulty and unhelpful thoughts, self-beliefs and uncomfortable emotions for almost four decades, causing my sense of self and reality to be skewed from who I really am. Negative emotions are a sticky trap and when we are under their influence, our outlook, the beliefs we form and our life experiences are all affected.

As soon as I saw the illusion, I was free from the trap.

This magnetic force attracts the same, rather than the opposite and becomes increasingly stronger along the continuum line in the direction of the polar ends, where emotions are at their strongest.

If the continuum line were curled to form a circle, the two ends would repel each other and would not meet. Deep misalignment and despair are vibrationally the opposite of happiness, joy and love. When in deep misalignment, the thoughts, ideas and beliefs we resonate with are the opposite of the those we resonate with when we are happy.

This force and illusion also influences our behaviours. Wherever we are along the continuum line provides us with force and impetus to engage in behaviours that match our emotional vibration.

Emotions influence the kinds of thoughts and behaviours we have, resonate with, believe and are drawn towards.

Put what I have presented within this chapter to the test and notice where your thoughts go when you feel good emotionally and if those thoughts seem true and believable. And notice where your thoughts go when you feel bad emotionally and if those thoughts seem true and believable.

Do you believe one set of ideas about yourself when you are misaligned and yet believe different ideas about yourself when you feel good emotionally?

Observe your perceptions and behaviours when you feel different emotions. This force and illusion is more noticeable when strong emotions are experienced.

Examples of the Magnetic Force and Illusion of Emotions

- Seeing the good in life when happy.
- Being driven and motivated to engage in life-enhancing activities when happy (for example: eating a good diet, exercising and socialising).
- Engaging in comfort eating or being drawn to 'unhealthy' food/drink when unhappy.
- Being easily startled when nervous.
- Having a tendency to withdraw and disengage from life-affirming activities when feeling depressed.
- Saying things in anger which are then regretted later when less angry.
- Smiling at a random stranger when in a good mood.

(The last two examples above also demonstrate the effects of this force and illusion rippling out and affecting others, as well as the individual.)

- Engaging in self-criticism when misaligned.
- Engaging in self-harm when feeling deep despair.

This chapter provides two points of the framework:

- **When the alarm is triggered, in addition to feeling bad emotionally, the magnetic force and illusion of emotions causes us to become caught in unhelpful cycles of thoughts, emotions, behaviours and beliefs.**

- **This, along with giving other false threats our attention, leads to what I refer to throughout *One Simple Step* as emotional issues and unnecessary emotional suffering.**

I shall now pull those eight main threads together.

CHAPTER 13

FRAMEWORK FOR UNDERSTANDING EMOTIONS

1. Negative emotions are an alarm when the true self is threatened.
2. Threats to the true self are either false or real.
3. False threats, which can include our own thoughts and behaviours, exist only when they have our attention.
4. Real threats exist whether they have our attention or not.
5. Beliefs form through repetition and regardless of how those beliefs feel.
6. When the alarm is triggered, in addition to feeling bad emotionally, the magnetic force and illusion of emotions causes us to become caught in unhelpful cycles of thoughts, emotions, behaviours and beliefs.
7. This, along with giving other false threats our attention, leads to what I refer to throughout *One Simple Step* as emotional issues and unnecessary emotional suffering.
8. When the body is not alerting us to threats, we are in our natural state, which is alignment: the emotions from hope, through to joy and beyond.

Understanding our emotions in this way leads to the method, which is simply to refrain from giving false threats our attention. When we do this, we heal emotionally and also eliminate point 6 above from our psyche and our experiences.

I shall now summarise this framework further and, in the next section, condense it into those three concise points.

PART III
EMOTIONAL HEALING THE EASY WAY

CHAPTER 14
THREE PIECES OF THE PUZZLE

All you need to know to practise the method is the following:

- Negative emotions are a warning signal when the true self is threatened.
- How to tell the difference between false threats and real threats.
- There is a magnetic force and illusion to emotions.

CHAPTER 15
ONE SIMPLE STEP

When you understand your emotions in this way, the one simple step to emotional healing is:

Turn away from false threats and do so in whatever way is right for you and the situation.

CHAPTER 16

SOMETHING WE ALL ALREADY DO ANYWAY

I call it a method for ease of reference, although it is something we all already do anyway.

What makes this simple action a healing system is choosing to understand your negative emotions according to this simple framework and therefore rejecting false threats more than you would otherwise do.

We turn away from false threats, heal emotionally and gain clarity on any real threats in our circumstances where they had been previously obscured.

There are endless distractions in our lives today, which can assist with turning our attention away from false threats.

When we practise this method and if there are no real threats in our circumstances, we experience the resulting lift of coming back into alignment anywhere between instantaneously and in the time it takes for the body to process and clear the negative emotions at a cellular level.

If your life is safe, stable and secure with no real threats and if you are living with emotional difficulties, then with this method, it is just one step to the sweet spot of life: no emotional issues, no life difficulties and your thoughts and beliefs singing in harmony with who you truly are.

That is life at its best.

CHAPTER 17
THE METHOD IN MORE DETAIL

When you turn away from the cause of your negative emotion and the negative emotion disappears, then you know the cause was a false threat.

When you turn away from the cause and the negative emotion persists, or your thoughts keep returning to the problem despite your repeated efforts to turn away from it, then you know the cause is a real threat to your true self.

How you respond to real threats is your individual choice and at your discretion and is not a part of this healing system. Responding to real threats may sometimes involve making and acting upon life-changing decisions. The only life-changing decision of this healing system is the one to turn away from false threats.

When you practise this method, you will get a feel for how quickly your negative emotions disappear when triggered by false threats and how persistently they linger when triggered by real threats. With clarity on real threats, you are less likely to internalise them as faults of yours and more likely to know how to deal with them.

When you are living through phases of real threats, practising this method can serve as a support through times when you might otherwise sink, along with any of the other endless supports that are available.

I discuss more about real threats in Part IV.

This method is not suitable for those living with symptoms of psychosis, which cause the individual to be detached from reality, or those living with the distressing symptom of ongoing uncontrollable and unwanted thoughts.

CHAPTER 18

LOGO

The simple pattern of the logo for this model is a visual aid to assist you in remembering this healing system. It combines the three pieces of the puzzle, the one-step method and how and when to practise it. (Please read the text in the four smaller circles from the top left circle and in a clockwise direction)

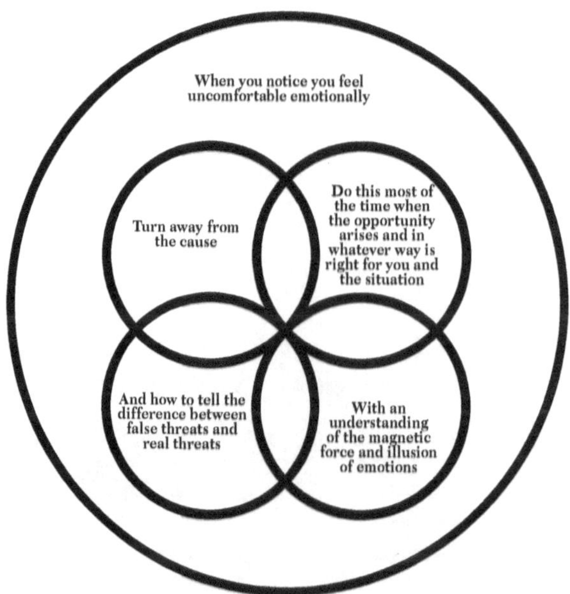

There is no need to remember the four smaller circles in any particular order, as they happen simultaneously when using the method in ordinary life.

CHAPTER 19

EXAMPLES OF THE METHOD IN ACTION

Clarity, Ease and Remaining Emotionally Well

Whilst chatting with a friend, I felt perfectly fine emotionally. I started to explain how when I was a kid, I was not as good at academics as my brother was and I felt intellectually inferior to him. Just seconds into explaining this, I noticed I started to feel misaligned.

With the warning noted, I ceased that line of discussion in a way that felt appropriate to the situation. I noticed my misalignment waned in seconds, just as quickly as it had arrived and I felt good again.

Even though I was talking about something from a long time ago, my body let me know that it is out of harmony with who I truly am to refer to myself as inferior to others.

Of course, the misalignment that was triggered could have been interpreted as stemming from unresolved issues, repressed emotions, buried trauma, or some other indication that I have more work to do on myself.

With my simple one-step approach however, I easily understood the reason for my misalignment, I was reminded of who I truly am and felt empowered and good again, all in a matter of seconds.

I understood the misalignment I felt to be a warning signal. When I took heed of the warning, the negative emotions, having done their job, diminished and disappeared.

We have our own inner therapist with us all of the time, within the information and guidance from our own negative emotions.

Eliminating the Confusion and the 'I Shoulds' and 'I Should Nots'

An individual who lived in different countries during childhood thrives on change and adventure as an adult.

In her midtwenties, she worked on a farm in New Zealand and, after six months, felt it was time to move on to a new adventure.

This person's employer interprets this love of change as an inability to settle and as a character flaw. The employer's comments were powerful and the individual decided to change her plans and stay on the farm longer to prove those comments were incorrect.

Her first six months there had been a wonderful time, whereas the following six months were different and filled with difficulties and problems.

There is no knowing what the alternate scenario would have been if the individual had kept to her original plans, as life has no control experiment. However, if the person had dismissed those false threat comments from her employer, she would have remained in the alignment, clarity and power of knowing who she truly is and would have eliminated the confusion, the self-doubt and the 'I shoulds' and 'I should nots' from that experience.

False Threats Can Be Debilitating

The following example is inspired by the film *I Am Ruth*:

A teenage girl has insecurities about her physical appearance. These insecurities have become beliefs which are often triggered and plague her mind and thoughts on a daily basis. She hears an unpleasant comment about her appearance which cuts deep and confirms what she already feels about herself. This is compounded by some unpleasant comments she reads on social media. She starts to become obsessed by her appearance, is self-critical and starts to fall into a hole of depression and self-hatred.

The girl becomes withdrawn; she loses interest in activities she used to enjoy; her family relationships become strained and fraught; and those close to her also start to get pulled into the black hole she has fallen into. The despair she is feeling and the critical self-beliefs that occupy her thoughts all feel very real and her mental health is highly worrying for her family.

The psychological self-hatred she is experiencing escalates into physical self-harm and other self-destructive behaviours.

The Foregoing Scenario with the Method

Although it was painful and felt very real, the self-loathing the girl felt was the result of the vortex created by false threats along with the power of the magnetic force and illusion of emotions.

If she had turned away from the false threats of put-downs, then this individual would be living a very different reality. The self-loathing thoughts and ideas would have been nipped in the bud and prevented from growing. By refusing to entertain or give airtime to these kinds of self-disapproving thoughts, she would have had the space to see her beauty and the wonder of her body and to experience any other empowering perceptions in alignment with her true, higher self.

It is these reaffirming thoughts that would then grow into beliefs and form her self-perception.

Using the Method in Circumstances of a Real Threat

An individual starts a new job. It is a great opportunity and in a field he is passionate about. However, the department is poorly managed and the new employee is not given an adequate induction or training and is plunged into the deep end with no support from a supervisor or manager.

This continues for weeks. The individual feels stressed and overwhelmed, his sleep becomes disrupted and he awakes in the night worrying.

Old self-beliefs that had lain dormant for years, beliefs surrounding inadequacy and not being good enough, become triggered. Because the person feels misaligned, he resonates with these thoughts and believes them.

If the individual had understood his emotions through the framework presented in *One Simple Step*, he would have understood the effects of his misalignment and could have filtered out the false threats. His days in this new role would still have been a challenge and he still would have experienced the stress of this. However, by eliminating the self-doubts and thoughts of inadequacy, the experience would have been far less disempowering and overwhelming.

The practice of this method is mostly simple, quick and easy. I shall now discuss those circumstances where it becomes more of a challenge.

PART IV
SPECIAL CONSIDERATIONS

CHAPTER 20
FALSE THREATS

I shall now look at circumstances where the practice of this method can become more of a challenge, looking at false threats in this chapter and real threats in the following two chapters.

When you are new to living by this method and experience feelings of misalignment that are intense, it can seem as though no healing has taken place. Old unhelpful beliefs can revive and become active once again and it can seem as though you are back to square one with the old identity and old psychological problems you used to live with.

This is purely the magnetic force and illusion of emotions at play wherever you are along the continuum line. Understand the illusion that is at play and continue to use the method.

As long as there is no real threat in your circumstances, you will experience yourself gradually moving along the continuum line in the direction of alignment and away from the place where the old disempowered you resides.

The pull on your attention from what is misaligned and the illusion of emotions can both be powerful forces, especially when emotions are strong. It is easier to go with this current than against it. However, if you choose not to get swept along by these forces when you feel misaligned and you resist the pull of the whirlpool when the forces are especially strong, you recover more quickly and prevent further misalignment for yourself and possibly others.

Resist the flow of the unhelpful current, resist the whirlpool and understand that any old unwanted thoughts patterns and beliefs are just the effects of the magnetic force and illusion of emotions on the misalignment you are feeling. If you resist the flow of that current and if there are no real threats, then you will move along the continuum line and into alignment.

Just as you would gauge your activities when healing from a physical injury, the same applies when healing from an emotional injury. Understanding your emotions from the perspective of this framework will help you be kind to yourself, draw support from that which matches your vibration and ensure you are not pushing yourself too quickly or putting unreasonable expectations on yourself.

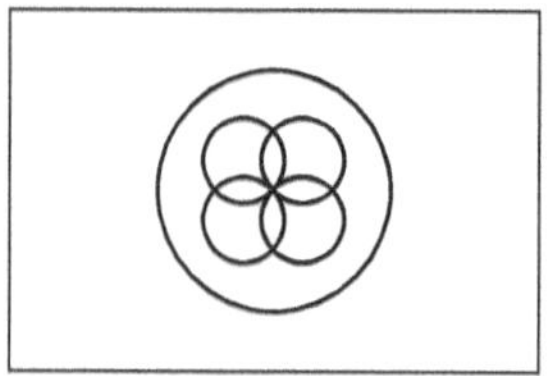

If misalignment and the force and illusion of emotions have gathered momentum and are a challenge to work against, sleep can provide a useful aid and reset and can also assist in distinguishing false threats from real threats.

If you are using this method and feel misaligned at the end of your day, then when you awake after sleeping and find the misalignment is gone, you know the misalignment was caused by a false threat. If you awaken and the misalignment continues, then you know it is being caused by a real threat to your true self.

This means that when you use this method, each day brings a new start. Sleep assists with the practice of the method, with the distinguishing between false threats and real threats and therefore with providing further clarity and understanding of who you truly are.

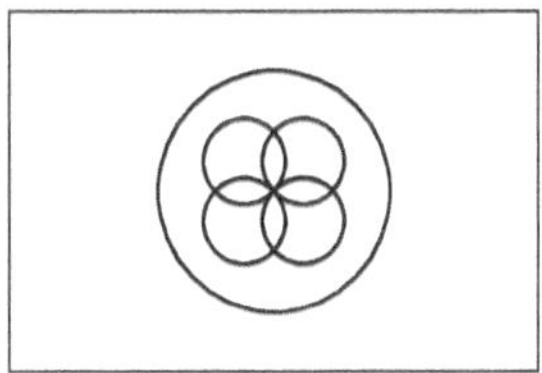

Utilising this information, amongst bringing many other benefits, enables you to shift your belief system and automatic thought processes in such a way that you become empowered and aligned with your true self. Without deliberate intention, you abandon, ditch, clear and let go of unhelpful self-beliefs that previously shaped you into a misaligned version of yourself. Instead, you re-set and re-wire your mind as self-beliefs that are aligned with what brings you happiness grow, develop and flourish — and your value no longer depends on the validation of others.

This is a method of aligning core beliefs: bringing the ideas and attitudes you hold about yourself and your life into a place that is attuned to your true self and to feelings of happiness, joy and love.

There may be some people in your world, however, who project onto you the old version of you they are more familiar with. Awareness of this phenomenon will provide you with a protective shield against their outdated perceptions.

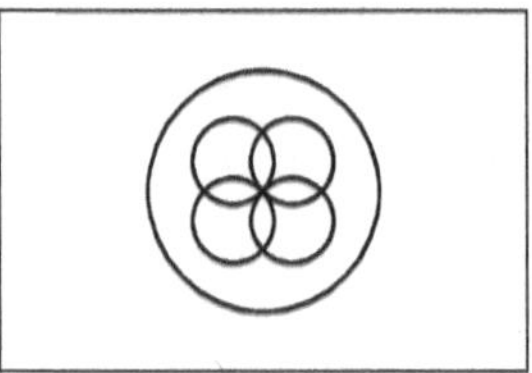

When false threats come along so frequently that batting them away becomes ineffective, they become a real threat. Just one real threat in our circumstances, no matter how small, will trigger the alarm of negative emotions.

CHAPTER 21

SPECIAL CONSIDERATIONS

If you are new to the teachings of *One Simple Step* and choose to give them a go, yet you are living through real threats, then the continued emotional discomfort you will be experiencing will likely cause you to lose interest in *One Simple Step* and its method, conclude it does not work and move away from it.

Before you disregard *One Simple Step*, suppose your emotion response is functioning perfectly well. Consider for a moment if there is an ongoing situation in your present life that may be misaligned with who you truly are.

Does that situation dim your light or enable you to shine?

Rather than translating your ongoing emotional discomfort as something wrong with you, as something you are prone to and as just the way you and things are, using this method will help you easily ditch any problematic emotional baggage you have been carrying around and give you clarity on the real threats amidst your circumstances.

When you do this, you gain the healing and you also gain the insight.

CHAPTER 22
REAL THREATS

Living through phases of real threats unfortunately seems an inevitable part of life. Sometimes real threats appear out of nowhere, sometimes they creep into our life gradually and sometimes they are of our own making, albeit unintentionally.

Some real threats change, pass, or resolve spontaneously. Some are within our control to change and others are not. Some are easy to resolve; others have no obvious solution; and some can feel like an insurmountable task. Whatever the cause of the problem, there is no guarantee that our attempts to improve our situation won't actually worsen it or get us into an even bigger mess. Because of this uncertainty, this healing system does not include how one responds to real threats.

What I offer in this chapter instead are points for consideration and insight into the effects on our emotions when we are living through phases when life is unkind.

Sometimes we live through phases of real threats, which cause a background misalignment in our everyday life. We function and have moments of alignment, although life in general feels like a struggle.

The misalignment may be a subtle flat feeling, a background stressed feeling, or a tired heaviness. However subtle, constant, or familiar the feeling, if in general we are not feeling hopeful, if we feel heavy and drained rather than light and lifted, then we are in misalignment and our true selves are not shining in an aspect of our lives or in our lives as a whole.

Sometimes we are faced with one real threat or several, a succession of one difficulty after another, a combination of false threats and real threats bombarding us from all angles. We may buckle under the weight of real threats and be back on our feet once they have passed.

There may be layers of real threats in our circumstances. One layer resolves in some way, only to reveal another situation that had previously been overshadowed but is out of harmony with who we truly are.

The list of scenarios unfortunately goes on and on. We weather the storms; we are resilient to many of the challenges life can bring; and we dig deep and find strength when we have to.

Utilising this method gives us clear visibility on the real threats to our true selves. With clear understanding, we are less likely to misinterpret our emotion response to these threats as faults or flaws.

Using the method can help us keep afloat through times when we might otherwise sink, along with any of the other seemingly endless ways we may dampen our internal alarm of a real threat.

There is a vast array of props and supports available in our lives today that can nurture us, nourish us and provide us with help, assistance, care and comfort when we are living through the difficulty of a real threat: talking with others who take time to understand us and our situation, socialising, spending time on our own, exercising, resting, spending time in nature, watching films, watching comedy, reading books, listening to music, observing silence, engaging in hobbies, practising mindfulness, practising meditation, practising visualisation, taking time to 'stop and smell the roses,' employing therapies, seeing our GP and seeking out support/social/advice services, to name but a few.

While we navigate through real threats, leaning on the support of this method, along with the good in life that is available, can ease the pain of the misalignment and the equation for happiness can look more like this:

Turn away from false threats, when there are no real threats = happiness

Nourish and nurture your true self when living through real threats = happiness

Emotions provide information on the safety of our true self and will indicate when the balance shifts and the good in your life outweighs the bad.

Sometimes, just simply resting in the knowing that life is presenting a difficulty and feeling emotionally rubbish is a natural consequence of that, is a choice that feels like the right one.

There are also, unfortunately, real threat circumstances where the good is insignificant compared to the pain of the misalignment.

PART V
MORE BENEFITS

CHAPTER 23
MORE BENEFITS

When we take heed of our inner voice of emotions and refrain from adding fuel to the fire of our own misalignment, we deflect the many false threats we might come up against through the many experiences of everyday life. We prevent the forming and strengthening of unhelpful beliefs and prevent ourselves from falling down endless rabbit holes of misalignment and possibly dragging others down into them with us.

The method becomes a backdrop to daily life, a way of living and responding to the vast array of experiences we encounter. Therefore, this is a method of emotional healing that takes no time to do.

It is an individual practice, depending upon each individual's emotion response and for this reason it empowers the individual to know, more than any other, what is right and what is wrong for him or her. With this, the individual understands more of who he or she truly is and with that comes the benefit of less pressure and fewer expectations on self to be or not be a certain way.

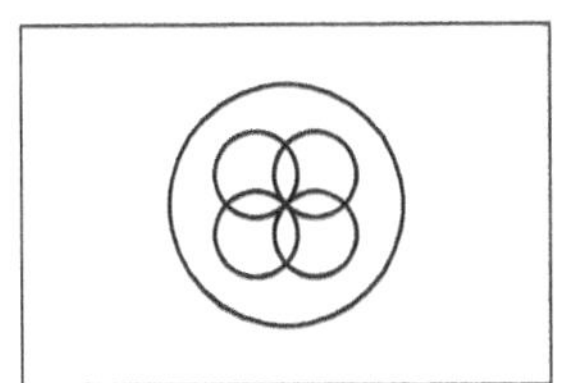

When we understand that our negative emotions are a warning signal, we find it much easier to avoid, dismiss, ignore, disregard, move or turn away from what does not serve us, including our own unhelpful thoughts.

Unwanted thoughts only seem true because of the negative emotions present with them — and maybe also because of the beliefs we have formed. Yet if we turn our attention away from those thoughts, then the negative emotions have done their job and they diminish and disappear.

Just like a spinning top, which when it ceases to be spun will lose momentum, slow down and stop, so too will the cycle and loop of negative thoughts and emotions, together with all the negative life experiences that would have been both a consequence of and also the power behind that spinning top.

When we experience phases of misalignment, we know it is because of misaligned life circumstances rather than anything fundamentally wrong with us or our psyches. We can also let ourselves off the hook, make life easier where we can and know we can shine easily again when our internal alarm signalling a real threat stops ringing.

Sometimes simply being consciously aware that the cause is a real threat is all that is required for the alarm of it to diminish and we learn more of what nourishes our souls and what does not.

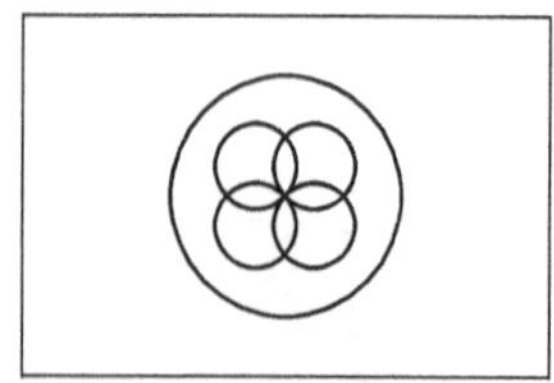

When we are aligned, because of the magnetic force and illusion of emotions, positive thinking becomes effortless. We believe in our hopes, dreams and goals and also in our ability to achieve them with ease and in the most joyful and aligned way.

Through the lens of alignment, the ordinary, the everyday and sometimes even the unwanted can be translated into what is wanted. And we may also find ourselves seeing the positive in surprising and unexpected places.

The powerhouse of the subconscious, the beliefs held there and the automatic thinking they provide then become ever more supportive.

This is the magnetic force and illusion of emotions working its magic. It happens as a natural side effect of happiness, just as perceived fears, doubts and worries can occur as a side effect of unhappiness.

We clear unnecessary misalignment and thereby enable more opportunities, when we are not faced with real threats, for the magnetic force and illusion of emotions to work more often in our favour. We enable this force to flow free and assist us when we are aligned and minimise its negative effects when we are misaligned; and we become the manipulator of energy, rather than having energy manipulate us.

When the unhelpful trap of the magnetic force and illusion of emotions becomes glaringly obvious, it also becomes no longer a part of our reality.

The ability of the mind to absorb what it has learnt causes this method to become second nature if you choose to practise it.

CHAPTER 24

HOW WE GOT OURSELVES INTO SUCH A PICKLE

Prior to this understanding we experience and through repetition form beliefs about our self, our place in the world and in relation to others, regardless of whether those beliefs are aligned with the true self or not.

The way the mind learns, along with the magnetic force and illusion of emotions, causes beliefs to grow and become strong and robust and ways of thinking to become engrained and entrenched. If those beliefs are misaligned, then cycles of unhelpful thoughts and painful emotions are set in motion.

Negative emotions can be misinterpreted, disregarded, ignored, overridden and overridden by what another thinks the individual should be feeling. The individual learns they and their emotions are faulty and along with the forming and strengthening of other misconceptions and disempowering self-beliefs, the individual lives de-railed from the power of who they truly are.

Even with an empowered and healthy sense of self, without an understanding of this framework, problems can still arise.

We all already follow the guidance of our negative emotions. We all already turn away from what triggers misalignment. We do this in whatever way is right for us and the situation and to some degree we understand the concept I have termed the magnetic force and illusion of emotions.

However, we only apply this concept and do this from time to time and only in a random and haphazard way.

We see the value in some of the negative emotions we feel and the guidance they are offering us, but sometimes we interpret these emotions as issues, flaws, hang-ups and something wrong with us.

Without an understanding of those three pieces of the puzzle, we may be giving some false threats our attention and unknowingly enabling them to grow, whilst taking measures to blot out the alarm of some real threats. Amidst all this chaos and confusion, false threats turn into emotional issues that we, and others, mistake as our identity. And we misinterpret our internal alarm indicating a real threat as something wrong with us. When we also consider the effects and trap of the magnetic force and illusion of emotions when we are misaligned, we find it no wonder that so many today are living with mental and emotional health difficulties.

We could become caught in tangles and loops of all kinds of misalignment, which can be a direct route to further misalignment. The emotional issues experienced by so many — including me before I discovered this information — could continue for months, years, decades, or even a whole lifetime, shaping and creating flawed self-beliefs, flawed perceptions, flawed experiences and a flawed life story, which were never even a part of who we truly are.

We learn through experiences that misalignment, in all its emotional, behavioural and physical manifestations, is normal and is just the way we are and we forget that happiness and shining our light is our natural state of being.

CHAPTER 25
EGO

This model for understanding the psyche does not include a separate unit to represent the ego. In this chapter, I offer an alternative way to understand this part of us and, with this understanding, bring it from the shadows and into the light.

The function of the ego is self-promotion. It is the driving force behind taking the ideas and creations from within to the outside world and therefore it assists and contributes to forward motion and progress.

When we respond to our negative emotions using this framework, the ego's role of self-promotion is channelled less often through misalignment. With this, there comes a sense of a diminishing ego, in the traditional understanding of it and the ego instead becomes elevated and valued for what it is: aligned with and an expression of the true self.

PART VI

WHEN THE METHOD BECOMES INEFFECTIVE

CHAPTER 26
WHEN THE METHOD BECOMES INEFFECTIVE

Leaning on what is available to you when living through the difficulties brought about by real threats can be useful in the short term until the threat passes. However, just as a ringing alarm will continue to ring even if the sound is muffled, so too will the alarm of a real threat.

If the alarm is set off too often or rings persistently it becomes a drain on our resources, including energy level, motivation and engagement and interest in life. It can also possibly deplete our health in terms of other body systems.

With the resulting drain, who we are becomes overshadowed by someone we are not.

Even with understanding your emotions with help from this guide and minimising unnecessary stress, worries, fears and unhappiness, living with one or more real threat, depending upon its nature, severity, or duration, can take you to the tipping point. It can cause your defences and resilience to weaken, can cause the walls to cave in on you, can even make you feel you are losing your grasp on reality and can back you into a hopeless and overwhelming corner.

When it feels that there is no escape from the circumstances of a real threat, one defence against the pain of the misalignment is to become emotionally numb — to function and exist, but be detached from one's emotions as a way of coping and surviving.

When misalignment is prolonged, continuous, extreme, or intense; when it feels there is no point in carrying on; when an individual is immobilised with the misalignment they feel; when an individual is resonating with suicidal thoughts; or when adjusting to a loss feels impossible, this method becomes ineffective and any benefits it may otherwise have are lost in the misalignment felt.

Within these realms, what is right or wrong for us becomes clouded and warped by the magnetic force and illusion of emotions and we lose sight of the clarity of knowing who we truly are.

Understanding the force and illusion that is working against us during such times can offer some insight. But the intensity of misalignment when beyond or teetering at the edge of that tipping point is outside the scope of what *One Simple Step* and its method are able to assist with.

Feeling bruised and battered emotionally with a weakened immunity to false threats and inevitably identifying with disempowered versions of the self may impact negatively on physical health too.

Crisis support professionals are there to help and provide support for such overwhelming difficulties.

PART VII
BRINGING IT ALL TOGETHER

CHAPTER 27
SUMMARY

I was in my early twenties when I realised I held beliefs that a person could heal from within. Since then, I have been navigated by this. First in a meandering way for eleven years, then with more focus and direction, with the past eight years being dedicated to my developing this work.

In 2016 ideas came to me of ways I could bring the beliefs I held into a better feeling place. I continued to refine the method from this starting point and continually sought truth and clarity on it. Sometimes inspired ideas flowed; sometimes they were silent; and over the course of the ensuing years the method gradually morphed and evolved.

Originally it was a way of intentionally creating and strengthening aligned beliefs through turning away from misaligned thoughts in meditation and visualisation. I then took this into one-to-one sessions with clients.

Just over a year later, it transitioned out of a sessions base and became a method we can apply and use as a backdrop to everyday life.

A practice that took place in the setting of a one-to-one session, took dedicated time and focus and only appealed to some, gradually morphed into a practice that takes no time and is accessible to and can be utilised by almost anyone.

However, the magic in this method was still elusive to those who read *One Simple Step*. Because of this, I knew there must be more for me to discover.

The pieces of the picture of negative emotions gradually came together, then moved to centre stage and became the framework for understanding emotions. The method gradually became a natural consequence of understanding our emotions in this way, and is simply to refrain from giving false threats our attention.

The framework for understanding emotions is condensed into three concise points and the one-step method provides the healing.

CHAPTER 28

AT A GLANCE

Understand emotions in this way:

- **Negative emotions are a warning signal when the true self is threatened.**
- **How to tell the difference between false threats and real threats.**
- **There is a magnetic force and illusion to emotions.**

You can be your happy true self more often by taking this one simple step - **turn away from false threats** - applied to everyday life, it looks like this:

CHAPTER 29
CONCLUSION — IT'S JUST AN ILLUSION

False threats are the cause of much emotional suffering in our world today and yet they only exist when we look at them.

Giving false threats our attention, the negative effects of the magnetic force and illusion of emotions, emotional issues and unnecessary emotional suffering are all illusions which cause us to live derailed from the power of our happy and vibrant true selves.

With this companion guide, you take one simple step out of the chaos and loop of perpetuating the unnecessary problems of false threats and instead face a whole new landscape where you allow your negative emotions to tell you of any problems, rather than allowing your thoughts to create such problems.

With a few pieces of information on negative emotions and a slight tweak to something you already do anyway, you can accurately understand the wisdom of your emotional self, align with your happy and vibrant true self and the thrill of this physical life experience and live with a stronger foundation through many of the real threats of life.

When you take heed of what your negative emotions are telling you, with an understanding of this framework, you easily, quickly and efficiently clear the layer of false threats from your experiences. You prevent yourself from falling into the trap of the magnetic force and illusion of emotions; gain a clear picture of what your negative emotions are telling you; and you gain the healing.

We learn the boundaries of what is acceptable to our true selves; become immune to absorbing, internalising and interpreting the vast variety of threats, both false and real, as weaknesses and faults; and eliminate 'I should' and 'I should not' from our self-talk.

When we banish false threats from our psyche and experiences, the only phases of misalignment are then the result of living through life's difficulties. With awareness of any real threats, we can continue to banish false threats and in doing so help keep ourselves afloat through challenging times. We do this along with using any of the other endless supports available that help turn down the sound of the alarm whilst we move through and respond to the inevitable stressors of life in any way we need or choose.

It is well known that stress plays a part in health problems and is linked to many physical ailments. Responding to the guidance of your negative emotions in this way is a fast-track route to stress reduction and all the benefits of health and well-being this brings.

The mind-body connection and the idea of the power within the mind to heal the physical body was the spark that ignited me the most when I was first drawn to self-healing. What I have discovered is that it is the body that has the ability to heal the mind.

Rather than ignoring, masking, or becoming caught in the tangle of negative emotions, we understand they are an indication, in this present moment, of what is not in harmony with our true selves and we gain access to the bigger part of who we are and become consciously awake to what we were previously sleepwalking through. Negative emotions then become indicators of what is not working for us rather than indicators of how we are not working.

The subconscious and belief system filter out what is not tried and tested and emotions filter out what is not a vibrational match. With one simple step, we place a filter over all these and filter out what is not useful. The way our minds learn and the magnetic force and illusion of emotions then do the rest of the work for us, working in our favour rather than against us.

As a by-product of utilising this method, you drop being the victim and being judgemental or jealous of others and instead master the art of letting go, forgiveness, rising above the inconsequential, we become genuinely happy for the success and alignment of others and function from what those in spiritual communities would call a higher vibration.

Self-beliefs become increasingly helpful where they were previously unhelpful. Living with our emotions becomes a whole lot easier and we step out of the quagmire of confusion and unnecessary difficulties and into a whole new happier and easier way of being.

CHAPTER 30
WHAT NOW?

It was about seven years ago when I started to intentionally turn away from triggers of misalignment in everyday life, rather than just in my meditation practice. Without realising it, I had found the method I had been searching for. Back then, though, my beliefs were such that I was not ready to accept emotional healing as being this simple.

You will be meeting this information with whatever your beliefs are about emotional healing. You are probably reading *One Simple Step* because you are living with emotional difficulties and would like to feel better. For these reasons and because it is so much easier to grasp these concepts when you observe them taking place within their original language of emotions, I invite you to trial this theory. Notice the outcome as compared with the outcome you would have experienced previously.

When you are aware of an uncomfortable emotion, cease the opportunity. Suppose your body is telling you the cause of the discomfort is a mismatch with your true self. Turn your attention away from that thought, subject, conversation, belief, or whatever it is, in whatever way is appropriate for you and the situation.

And see what happens …

Does the negative emotion disappear?

Do you feel good again?

AFTERWORD

When I started writing *One Simple Step*, I had just a basic plan, a vague outline and a strong sense that there was a purpose to this writing. I was unaware of the details, what the content of the book was to be, where the finish line was, or even if there was a finish line. This work has evolved through a great many revisions since it first started coming into my thoughts.

Compelled like a scientist seeking to find the equation, I continued on.

I observed the patterns and discovered the difference between false threats and real threats. I also observed how negative emotions affect our outlook and cause unhelpful thoughts, ideas and beliefs to seem true. With these discoveries, my old wounds healed, I banished unhelpful thinking patterns from my psyche and I was able to avoid the pitfalls of unhelpful thinking I so easily fell into in the past.

The first couple of years of this work were what my dreams were made of with the many joyous sessions and the process of writing was so easy that *One Simple Step* seemed to be writing itself.

However, there were times when I doubted what I was doing and where this was leading. This information was just coming from me after all and how my feelings respond.

In those earlier years, my daughter, six when this venture started, showed me her belief in this work. She understood the essence of it like no other and also understood how useful to others I was hoping this would be. When I was unsure of what I was doing, she would occasionally come out with some magical gem. With those few sweet words of encouragement or with a loving gesture regarding this work, she shined a light on the path for me to follow when I needed it.

My enquiry then led me round a corner and understanding misalignment further, with all its grittiness and nuances, then became the unexpected focus. Life experiences and difficulty with this writing then gave me plenty of opportunities to experience and examine misalignment of both kinds and in varying degrees of depth and intensity. I thought *One Simple Step* was finished, but with this unexpected change of direction, it had only really just begun.

A succession of real threats to my true self then gave me my teaching. I used the method as a safety harness, rather than relying on other supports and props, as I nudged myself along this precarious and what felt to be way too long exploration. This work dragged on and on and I started to doubt, like those around me already had, if *One Simple Step* would ever be finished.

I moved through a process of dives into misalignment. I experienced the pain, went to depths I had never been to before, looked around, posed questions, found a piece of the puzzle and understood more of how this method fit into the bigger picture of misalignment. Then I came back up again into more comfortable feelings for a breather. With each of these insights, I felt the lift of thinking: I had reached the finish line which I could not see.

Sometimes the dive was just minutes or hours and sometimes days, sometimes providing just part of a sentence and other times giving rise to a whole new chapter.

My heart goes out to those spending a longer time at those painful depths.

I was driven by my dream of finding an easy and enjoyable way to heal emotionally. I was unaware this meant bringing turning away from triggers of misalignment safely into ordinary everyday life. All of this essential, it turns out, in giving me the experiences needed to uncover this completed book, learn the scope of it, learn when its method becomes ineffective and be at peace with that.

Despite the challenges, this work has given me a sense of purpose like no other work has. And with my utilisation of this method, when I have not been living through real threats, feelings of happiness and clarity within my mind and body similar to those experienced when I practised meditation. My energy levels have increased; my immune system seems stronger; my physical and mental health have improved; and my mind and body feel clear, all at a time of life when the opposite is often true.

With the improvements to my physical health since practising this method, even with the stress of living through real threats over those last several years, I cannot help but wonder if there is a connection between immunity to false threats and the strengthening of the physical immune system.

Your life becomes easier and your soul nourished
a whole lot more, when you understand your
negative emotions are a warning signal.

ABOUT THE AUTHOR

With an interest in understanding emotions, behaviours and how to heal her own wounds, **Beth Kearney** began training in hypnotherapy in her early thirties.

Twenty years later, *One Simple Step* was finished.

www.ingramcontent.com/pod-product-compliance
Lightning Source LLC
Chambersburg PA
CBHW031413250726
48656CB00002B/659